Jason Thomas Wilmans

Agent-Based Simulation in Finance

Jason Thomas Wilmans

Agent-Based Simulation in Finance

An Application of Agent-Based Computational Economics Models to the U.S. Banking Market

Reihe Gesellschaftswissenschaften

Impressum / Imprint
Bibliografische Information der Deutschen Nationalbibliothek: Die Deutsche Nationalbibliothek verzeichnet diese Publikation in der Deutschen Nationalbibliografie; detaillierte bibliografische Daten sind im Internet über http://dnb.d-nb.de abrufbar.
Alle in diesem Buch genannten Marken und Produktnamen unterliegen warenzeichen-, marken- oder patentrechtlichem Schutz bzw. sind Warenzeichen oder eingetragene Warenzeichen der jeweiligen Inhaber. Die Wiedergabe von Marken, Produktnamen, Gebrauchsnamen, Handelsnamen, Warenbezeichnungen u.s.w. in diesem Werk berechtigt auch ohne besondere Kennzeichnung nicht zu der Annahme, dass solche Namen im Sinne der Warenzeichen- und Markenschutzgesetzgebung als frei zu betrachten wären und daher von jedermann benutzt werden dürften.

Bibliographic information published by the Deutsche Nationalbibliothek: The Deutsche Nationalbibliothek lists this publication in the Deutsche Nationalbibliografie; detailed bibliographic data are available in the Internet at http://dnb.d-nb.de.
Any brand names and product names mentioned in this book are subject to trademark, brand or patent protection and are trademarks or registered trademarks of their respective holders. The use of brand names, product names, common names, trade names, product descriptions etc. even without a particular marking in this works is in no way to be construed to mean that such names may be regarded as unrestricted in respect of trademark and brand protection legislation and could thus be used by anyone.

Coverbild / Cover image: www.ingimage.com

Verlag / Publisher:
AV Akademikerverlag
ist ein Imprint der / is a trademark of
OmniScriptum GmbH & Co. KG
Heinrich-Böcking-Str. 6-8, 66121 Saarbrücken, Deutschland / Germany
Email: info@akademikerverlag.de

Herstellung: siehe letzte Seite /
Printed at: see last page
ISBN: 978-3-639-49113-5

Contents

1 Motivation

Endogenous shocks and orthodox economics In the highly industrialized world we live in, the economy affects nearly every aspect of life - at least indirectly. Logically, a lot of effort was invested into economic sciences to understand and explain the basic rules of our economic systems. Yet, despite many observed severe, economic shocks throughout history, only relatively few theories even attempt to explain the fluctuations of varying amplitudes which are observable in any real market.

In fact, most macro economists rely on a highly formalized (general) equilibrium framework, where high fluctuations are conceived as rather unusual deviations from the norm. Those deviations are then explained by for example lags of propagation of new facts like a good's new price or shipment quantity (Carlton, 1983; Zarnowitz, 1962). Those "orthodox" models are being increasingly criticized by some not to predict, or even explain, fluctuations "out of themselves" (endogenously):

"[The model] does not contain an explicit theory of business cycle dynamics, because the economy rests in the steady state unless it is hit by some exogenous stochastic shocks. It does therefore not explain the movements of the business cycle endogenously. It rather generates its dynamics with a sort of 'deus−ex−machina mechanism' ..." [Fagiolo and Roventini 2008 cited in (Oeffner, 2008, p. 33)].

Understanding how and why these shocks occur would be extremely useful, to control the damage made or maybe even prevent them by improving the systems at work. But:

"Research on the origin of instabilities, overinvestment and subsequent slumps has been considered as an exotic side track from the academic research agenda (and the curriculum of most economics programs). This, of course, was because it was incompatible with the premise of the rational representative agent. This paradigm also made economics blind with respect to the role of interactions and connections between actors (such as the changes in the network structure of the financial

industry brought about by deregulation and introduction of new structured products). Indeed, much of the work on contagion and herding behavior (see Banerjee, 1992, and Chamley, 2002) which is closely connected to the network structure of the economy has not been incorporated into macroeconomic analysis." (Colander et al., 2009, p. 14).

However, in reality, fluctuations are an every day observation. And very strong shocks seem to occur quite often, as well. The latest examples are the burst of the dot com bubble in 2000 and the sub-prime mortgage crisis, which were only 7 years apart. Only a small minority of economists reportedly predicted the soon to be worldwide economic crisis, induced by an increase of sub-prime mortgage defaults in 2007. Those who did were ridiculed as "Dr. Doom" by the media or even literally laughed at, because it seemed so improbable to most economists (Fishman-Lapin, 2006; Nutting, 2006-08-23).

The few correct predictions that were cast, were also attacked for being either relatively late before the actual event, or earlier but quite inaccurate. Also, often there were no scientific papers published. What may be even more important is that of the known predictors, nobody (to my knowledge) based his claims on a formalized economic model, that could be used for further research.

Agent-based Computational Economics (ACE)   Since the upcoming of powerful information systems within the last few decades, there is the option of investigating market and economic behavior differently than before. Computer simulations of an unprecedented scale are now possible. While many rely on the well known, highly mathematically formalized (general) equilibrium frameworks with a single, representative, rational agent, others are searching for a different approach. Some economists are trying to model micro- and macro-economies as complex, non-linear systems. These models often rely on multi-agent settings and introduce other interesting notions that oppose the orthodox rational agents concept. There are a number of macroeconomic models, some with a general, stylized approach e.g. those by Leijonhufvud (2006) or Oeffner (2008). Others try to employ specific properties of real economies, for example the EURACE project (Cincotti et al., 2010), or the Aspen simulation (Basu et al., 2001). There is also a relatively great number of financial market simulations (Anufriev & Hommes (2012); Arthur et al. (30.11.1996); Hommes (2006a,b)). Curiously, I found few work on models of actual bank's behavior in order to test, for example, banking regulation policies. The only one is a study for the OECD (Thurner, 2011).

Purpose and goals   The main goal of this thesis is to examine and model banking behavior in the financial market, with a focus on credit holder constellations and to identify system conditions (related to the ownership constellations) that lead to market instability. For this purpose, a multi-agent-based economic model of banks and the institutions and actors they interact with is built. It is supposed to be a detailed model of the U.S. banking market that integrates some of the aforementioned theories. The sub models of the parts may be very rudimentary, as banks interact with a multitude of partners. A strong indicator of success would be, if the model, correctly parameterized and initialized with data from 2000, was able to predict a crash similar to the real one 2007, at a time somewhere around the exact historical events.

The ultimate goal was fulfilled only partly, due to three main factors. The most important one is simply the complexity of the matter. Banks operate exactly in the middle of processes on the macro- as well as on a micro-level. They interact with virtually every part of the economy in one way or the other, making it necessary to model each of those parts at least in a sketchy way. The different parts require a certain knowledge, that was cumbersome to obtain. The second reason is, that a lot of the data one would naturally gather to get an insight on a topic, are impossible to collect, even for the market participants themselves. The third problem was, that I was not able to find as many agent-based models, which actually refer to the real U.S. market, as I expected in the research phase. As a consequence, many of the model parts are original research or a really wide transfer of abstract theories to the real market situation. All factors combined consumed a lot more time than planned.

As a consequence, some parts are missing, which is why it cannot be implemented fully at this point in time, thus making calibration and validation impossible. However, it is a non-contradictory base so far, with most of the parts modeled, that could be completed and analyzed.

Thesis structure   Since a lot of the more in-depth terminology and structural knowledge used in this work is not common to members of the computer science academia, chapter two explains the important economic basics in a rather brief overview. This includes which actors are there in the financial system and how they are related. Chapter three introduces the general idea of bounded rationality which is at the very core of many developments in the ACE community, as well as more specific ACE models that were used in the simulation model. In chapter four, the actual simulation model is presented, first with an overview over all model elements, followed by the in-depth details of the separate elements. The outlook chapter, number five, gives a brief description on open research questions and possible improvements to the model. Chapter seven closes the thesis with a short conclusion.

2 Economic basics

2.1 Banking in a modern currency system

Creation of money and debt

To understand how the modern banking systems work, one has to let go of the ideas of what money is and how banks work, that were taught in school. Historically, money was an obligation for the bank printing it, to exchange a referenced resource worth the printed amount of the bank note to the customer, whenever he demanded it. Technically, one could reference any scarce resource. Some historical money systems referred to gold and silver and even seashells as a base value.

People or companies earned money by providing (mostly) goods and deposited most of it at their bank. Because normally the bank's customers do not demand all their money at the same time, the bank can then lend *fractions* of those deposits to business partners in return for interest payments. A part of the yield is payed to the depositors, to make depositing money more attractive. The value of the money was, next to other factors, reliant on the bank's ability to fulfill the promise of exchanging the money for the referenced good. For a long time it was also common, that each bank printed its own money.

Problems with physically bound currencies

This definition of money and debt held obvious advantages compared to a barter economy. Even as civilizations became a lot more developed than the societies that first introduced these concepts, similar systems were common until relatively recently in the human history. In the United States of America and other countries, that tied their currency to the U.S. dollar under the Bretton-Woods system, the currencies were connected to precious metals until U.S. President Richard Nixon outlawed the convertibility of dollars in August 1971.

Discussions about the usefulness and stability of different money systems surface until today. But what is indisputable is, that in a currency system, that is fixed to an amount of a physical reference (such as gold), the value of the money closely correlates with the physical availability of the referenced resource. Over- or under-supply of the resource change the money's value, regardless of the real economic situation. Additionally, since every material on earth is finite, so is the total volume of money referencing this value, potentially limiting economic growth. This property allows only limited control over the volume of money in circulation, which most of economists see as an indispensable tool for the stabilization of economies.

Since most economists attribute the occurrence of multiple economic crises at least partially to these properties, other systems were derived. Today, money is something quite different. The system in most of the developed countries works as follows.

"Modern" money

First of all, there are now generally two kinds of money: Central bank money and credit money. Both of these money types' value is not linked to the value of any physical reference anymore. There is no other security backing central bank money, than the receiving party's trust in its purchasing power. To strengthen the value of the money, there is normally only one legal currency allowed in a country. Credit money is slightly different from central banks money, because it is created from credit. This will be explained in a moment. The printing of physical money is restricted to a very narrow group of institutions (commonly federal[1] or supranational[2]).

M0	All physical money (Federal Reserve Notes + US Notes + Coins) in circulation (excluding those in Federal Reserve Banks or depository institution vaults)
MB	Monetary base, M0 + (excess) reserves in bank vaults and Federal Reserve Deposits
M1	M0 + demand deposits + NOW and similar interest-earning checking accounts
M2	M1 + savings deposits and money market deposit accounts + Small time deposits + retail money market mutual fund balances (excluding Keogh and IRA retirement programs, and only if < 100,000$)
M3	M2 + large time deposits + institutional money market mutual fund balances + repurchase agreements + Eurodollars
M4	M3 + commercial paper + Treasury-Bills

Figure 2.1: categorization of loans

---

[1]Federal Reserve System
[2]European Central Bank

However, in contrast to the historical system, physical currency, even combined with account balances is by far the smallest fraction of money in circulation anyway. In economics, "money" is not such a definite term as in colloquial speech[3]. Instead there are rigid definitions of multiple "money aggregates". The money aggregates as in use by the Federal Reserve System are stated in figure 2.1. A money aggregate is a group of value holding (not necessarily physical) entities in circulation within an economy, such as account balance, paper bills or stocks. The classification of the money aggregates depends mostly on the liquidity of the entities within each aggregate[4]. Apart from slight definition differences per country, they are substantially similar. The sum of M1 (i.e. what one would commonly regard as "money") made up only less than 13 % of M3 as reported by the Federal Reserve Board (16.03.2006)[5]. It is controversial as to what extent a money aggregate can be called "money", but there are also even broader definitions (e.g. M4). Still, all money aggregate's worth is denominated in U.S. dollars.

Fractional reserve banking   The central bank can, at least indirectly, influence the money supply. The different ways of interaction are illustrated in figure 2.2. It can create credit money "ex nihilo", simply by extending its balance sheet with amount x and rising a reserve account balance by x. Through this operation, the central bank creates new money and brings it into circulation[6]. The creation of money happens either, if this sum is a loan for the institution owning this account, or the central bank buys securities (in the USA often federal bonds). To achieve the opposite effect, the central bank can try to lower the money supply by selling securities it holds and shortening its balance sheet by the value of those securities, effectively destroying money.

Private banks can lend the central bank's money by contracts with a small[7] interest rate on extremely short terms (overnight to around two weeks). Commercial banks themselves are

---

[3]Within a fractional reserve banking system, which is being described at the moment.

[4]Liquidity is the term for the property of the entity, as to how fast it can be converted to "conventional" purchasing power. For example, a dollar bill is the most liquid there is, whereas a share in a mutual fund takes a significant amount of time to monetize.

[5]The last report including M3, since the Federal Reserve System stopped tracking this money aggregate in 2006.

[6]The argument is brought forward, that the money supply is in fact expanded by more than x. This theory is called multiplier effect. It suspects that, because after the commercial bank has this money in its books, it is allowed to lend more itself. If the party, that receives this loan is a commercial bank, it allows this bank to grant loans to another bank, and so on. However its not thoroughly accepted. *"[...] as discussed [...], the deposit multiplier is a myth. [...] broad monetary aggregates are created by banks as a function, almost exclusively, of their attitude towards credit risk, without narrow aggregates imposing any effective constraint."* Benes & Kumhof (2012)

[7]The Federal Reserve uses the term "discount rate". Actually there are three different programs (primary, secondary and seasonal credit) for commercial banks. Due to the Federal Reserve's strategy of "quantitative easing", which can be described as an excessive expansion of the money supply, these rates have been on historically low levels since 2008. The primary credit discount rate is at the time of writing this thesis at 0.75%.

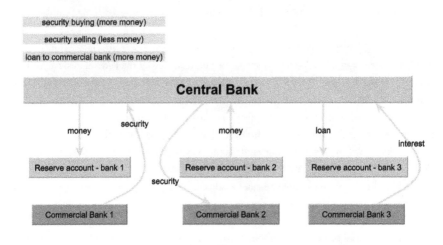

Figure 2.2: Fractional reserve banking and credit money

often also allowed to create money. When a customer requests a loan and the commercial institution grants it, the bank extends its own balance sheet by this amount and creates the credit volume on the customer's account. In this case, the money is backed by the borrower's promise to pay the loan plus interest back. That is why its called credit money. If the loan is paid back as expected, the basic credit volume is eliminated from the bank's balance sheet, but it retains all interest that was paid.

In contrast to the central bank, commercial banks are (theoretically) not allowed to create infinite amounts of money. Instead, they can expand their balance sheet (and thus the volume of money) only by lending new money to a customer. The maximum amount of money a financial institution is allowed to lend is limited by financial regulations . The reserve requirement (or liquidity ratio) determines the minimal fraction of the overall deposits, that a commercial bank must hold as a reserve, either physically in a vault or as deposits on accounts at the Federal Reserve System. In the United States, the minimum reserve requirement is staggered according to the bank's size, but for the biggest banks this value is 10%[8]. Its lending volume is regulated indirectly. That means that in contrast to the historical model a bank can expand its lending volume to a size 10 times as much as its reserves .

---

[8]In the Eurozone it is even lower with 1%.

2.1.1 Fields of business today

Since the first occurrences of money and banks, the credits and customer accounts have remained principal business segments for banks. Similar to the developments in the rest of the economy, the services in this area have become numerous and more diversified. A brief overview of the field is given in the next segment. But in the last decades, the banks sought new possibilities to make trade. Today, there are four areas in which banks engage besides giving credit. The first of those revenue streams are fees on offered services. Since those play only a minor role in the current revenue streams and are also fairly transparent, there is no further explanation on this topic. But the other three are introduced more extensively, since they will play a role in the simulation model.

Financial asset management   The first one will be summarized under the term "financial asset management". The volume of individual wealth has risen to heights, where it is beyond the holder's capacity (or will) to manage its investment themselves. Banks target this "high-net-worth individuals" (HNWI) with several strategies. There are bank branches or dedicated banks who focus on serving HNWIs with a higher personnel to customer ratio. These staff focus on giving investment proposals or completely managing the customer's assets. This is either done on a "per customer" basis, or to allow the customers to profit additionally from group advantages, there are also dedicated, collective investment schemes, with a professional manager and further employees who serve exclusively this target. Due to the different preferences of customers for investment strategies in terms of expected profits, risk management or diversification, these companies often differ significantly in size and performance characteristics - from relatively restricted (mutual) investment funds to nearly unregulated hedge funds. Not all of those financial vehicles belong to banks, but through more or less transparent networks, most banks engage increasingly in this sector. In fact, banks have already taken the lead regarding the size of hedge funds (Pasha (2006); Sorkin (2007)).

Traditional investment banking   Additionally to the rising relevancy of asset management, there is still a "classical" definition of investment banking. The main activities in this area are helping customers with security issuance (underwriting), brokerage (bundling of buy and sell operations of financial securities for easier access and reduced costs), and "Mergers & Acquisitions" advisory (as well as financing). Despite significant slumps in earnings following the financial crisis, "classical" investment banking, in combination with an increasing share of financial asset management, "still makes up the bulk of banks' income." Reuters (29.02.2012). However, the loan business stays an important factor in bank earnings.

Structured products   The last important source of bank revenue is the construction and selling of financial products. A structured product can be described as a security, whose value depends on the performance of one or more underlying securities. In common practice, these underlyings are often not under ownership of the institution issuing the structured product. The architecture and ownership constellations of some of those products (in combination with other factors) are believed to have been an important factor in the financial crisis that started 2007 (Brunnermeier, 2009; Colander *et al.*, 2009). I will now explain the most prominent specimen, which are used in nearly every explanation of the credit crunch in 2007. The most used financial derivatives in the explanations are Credit Default Swaps (CDS) and several kinds of Asset Backed Securities (ABS).

A CDS is a contract between issuer and buyer that defines a referenced entity (normally a corporation or a sovereign), an underlying debt by the referenced entity, credit events (e.g. delayed payments, issuer bankruptcy), a periodic premium and the settlement. The buyer agrees to pay a periodic premium (spread) (and often an initial fee) to the issuer. In return, the issuer guarantees to fulfill a "physical" or "cash" settlement towards the buyer, in case one of the named credit events occurs. In a "physical" deal, the seller obliges himself to buy the debt at par value from the buyer. Since there was a credit event, the market price of the securities is likely to be way below the face value. As a consequence, the buyer loses less money from holding the debt. In the cash option, the issuer pays the buyer the difference between the market price and the par value of the underlying. This is most often the case, if the buyer does not own any of the debt in any form.

There is an important detail, that differentiates a CDS from a regular insurance, although it may look like one at first sight. Neither its issuer nor its buyer have to be somehow related to the debt. Therefore, while a CDS contract can be used to hedge against debt risk, it can also be used to bet against the referenced entity. The protection promised by credit default swaps also tends to be more fragile than buyers expected, because they rely mainly on the liquidity of its issuer. If the CDS' seller accumulated unsafe risk distributions, the protection may as well be worthless, as seen with many institutions, for example AIG (Brunnermeier, 2009). Judging such risk, however, is impossible, since the exact holdings of securities or company debt is nontransparent to other market participants. This is true for "normal" debt directly to commercial banks, but even more for the "over-the-counter"[9] markets, since there are no

---

[9]Where the structured products, described in this paragraph, are traded.

reporting obligations at all, as to what debt belongs to whom.

Asset Backed Securities are commercial papers that are, as the name says, backed by a pool of assets. Their purpose (from the issuers view) is to move credit risk from its issuer towards the ABM's buyer. ABS' do not sell the assets itself, but payments from the pool of underlying assets. The exact specification of that pool is determined by the issuer. Often the assets in the pool stem from a certain category of loans, for example the most frequent one is home equity loans. But there are also products that pool, say, credit card loans with student loans and others. Depending on the exact nature of the underlyings they may be called differently.

Most relevant for this thesis are ABS' that are organized as Collateralized Debt Obligations (CDOs). Unlike most other financial products, they work in an algorithmic way. The flow of money from the underlying debt is paid out in different tranches. The number of tranches and their names vary, but often there are senior, mezzanine and junior tranches. The payments are spread over the tranches in such a way, that first all keepers of senior tranches are paid, only if there is something left the mezzanine, and finally the junior tranches. This results in a non-linear behavior of the payments and, of course, different risk profiles for the tranches. A now infamous variance of CDOs are real estate backed mortage securities (RBMS), especially those with a high fraction of subprime[10] customers.

The descriptions in this paragraph are extremely simplified and only intend to give a basic understanding of the topic. The real market is more complicated. There are numerous variations in durations, the nature of the underlyings, pooling of underlying assets and every other detail of such contracts. Also it is common practice to make lots of combinations of such structured products. To name only one example, there are such things as CDO^2 [11] and even CDO^3.

2.1.2 Credit types and corresponding customers

This section will give a short overview on the different credit customers and the credit forms that banks extend to them. For this thesis I am going to distinguish the customers into these categories: private households, corporate customers, other banks and public customers, namely the federal government or states and communes. During my research for this thesis, I

---

[10] Applicants for mortgages with a low FICO score. FICO is a private company that tries to asses private credit reliability, much like the german SCHUFA.
[11] A CDO with an underlying pool that includes CDOs.

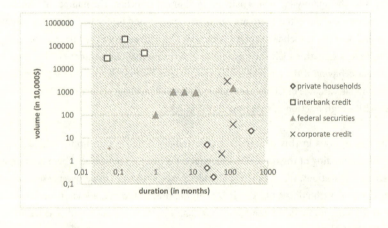

Figure 2.3: credit types by volume and duration (exemplary, not real data)

found that the level of available information is extremely diverse, depending on the target group. Public financing is (naturally) very well documented by official sources. Also, there are some useful studies regarding private households' behavior on that topic. But I was unable to find statistics about the strategies, mobility and preferences of corporations on the credit market. And when or how much or how often banks lend money to each other seems to be kept secret more or less actively.

The credit types with which banks deal have different forms, because its customers are very diverse. Figure 2.3 is an illustration to get an impression for how much the products vary (note the logarithmic scale). Credit contracts can also be securitized or not. The contract's duration varies largely, even for the same customers. There is the option of credit lines with a fixed upper border of total debt with an open end, or a loan with fixed end date. The duration for fixed end loans varies from "overnight" loans between banks with large sums to 30 year mortgages or government bonds.

Private households Private household debt in the United States is commonly high. From around 1985, where the debt to GDP ratio was around 48% it rose steadily, taking a rapid acceleration after 2000 to a peak of circa 95% in early 2009. After the recession it started falling quite sharply, marking approximately 78% as of date (Federal Reserve Bank St. Louis, 2013). Private households request a whole variety of credits. The market segment with the biggest volume by far is the mortgage sector. One can identify at least two different patterns of credit use. The first one is a special acquirement, financed (at least partially) by a credit, which is tried to pay off completely. This is very common with the important role of mortgages, but also for student or auto loans. Especially in the United States it is also very wide practice of customers maxing out their credit line to pay for everyday needs, especially in times of irregular income or unexpected medical costs Traub & Ruetschlin (22.05.2012).

Bank accounts are widely spread, but still a significant share of citizens have none or use their services only occasionally. According to (Federal Deposit Insurance Corporation, 2012), those households make up around 20.1% of U.S. households. Credit cards play a large role in their financial transactions and saving.

Corporations and small businesses Big companies and small businesses behave relatively different from one another. Aggregate data for small businesses was available from the U.S. Census Bureau until the government shutdown in late 2013. Small businesses rely on a very small number of capital sources, often a single business credit card line or relatively small loans. Unless they reach a certain size, they apply very earmarked for concrete projects. Banks also tend to demand collateralization of the applying business' assets. Since especially small businesses have trouble finding financing at all (even before the crisis), they are relatively immobile in terms of switching their financial institution. Also they generally do not have the man power to monitor the market and scan it for financing opportunities.

Unfortunately, I was unable to find any reliable sources for statistics about the behavior of financing and capital acquirement in really big corporations. The following information stems from non-scientific sources and a short, unofficial talk with an industry expert. It thus may be inaccurate or incorrect, but due to the lack of better sources, guessing is the best possible option so far. Still some things are logically deducable. Large companies have enough manpower to dedicate a group of staff to financing. Those departments are often even called treasuries. They are well informed about banking practice, often with a background in banking themselves. Also the financial volume of the company gives them a lot more weight in negotiations in comparison with small businesses. As far as my information goes, this is the main reason why companies seem not as likely to switch within banks as one would expect. Instead of scanning for the best offers and changing a single bank often, they are said to rely on multiple sources of income flow and use their importance to bargain attractive conditions. This is also supported by the fact, that negotiations about a US$200 million credit take significantly longer time and investigating effort, than a US$20,000 loan to a small business.

According to my information, really big corporations do not only diversify their sources of credit, but also the type. "Special purpose" credits, mostly securitized, are done for so called "movable assets", which means that those assets are potentially easy to monetize. Examples for that are airplanes, ships, but also buildings that could be sold, or even power plants that companies build near to their production facilities. But the majority of credit volume is made strategically for "general funding purposes", often unsecured except for the company's size and (maybe) good ratings. Also this demand for credit is said to be driven largely by strategic goals and only secondarily influenced by the interest level (extreme values excluded). However some middle- to long-term decisions with larger sums than usual might be advanced or postponed with the interest level in mind.

Federal government Normally, public customers, such as federal governments, states and local governments, do not borrow debt directly from financial institutions. Instead, the

U.S. Department of Treasury issues several kinds of bonds. Although there are some slight variations, most of those bonds are similarly designed. Each bond has a par value (often of US$1000). The bonds are sold (or auctioned) under par value, with the issuer promising to buy the bond back at par value when the bond has matured. If the difference between the paid price at issuance and the par price is greater than the money loss by inflation over the maturity time, this effect alone has generated wealth for the buyer. Additionally it is common, that the government pays regular fees to the holders of its securities. The maturity times vary from 28 days to around 30 years.

But banks do buy and trade these securities. According to the U.S. Department of the Treasury (2013), roughly 12% of the U.S. public debt were held by insurance companies, depository institutions and "other investors". So, indirectly, the federal government borrows money from those institutions. Also, there are more public customers from states to local governments and cities.

2.2 Hedge funds

Hedge funds are a really important part of the financial market nowadays. They are private investment funds with a special legal status, exclusively for HNWIs (High-net-worth-individuals). In contrast to "normal" investment vehicles, the minimum share to become a customer is very high; usual are figures around $1 million. This is due to regulation, as well as the target group of investors. For example, U.S. based hedge fund investors have to be "qualified investors" which means, that they have to have a certain net value and yearly income. There are many different legal forms that allow the funding of hedge funds, on which I will not go into detail. But there are three most important features of a hedge fund in contrast to, say, a mutual fund.

One: hedge funds for a long time did not have any, and still have few, third party reporting obligations at all. In recent times, the U.S. Security and Exchange Commission (SEC) is addressing this situation increasingly. Since the 2010 Dodd-Frank Wall Street Reform Act, U.S. based hedge funds with assets under management (AUM) worth more than US$150 million, more than 15 investors or a single investor with more than US$25 million in the fund must register with the SEC and file regular reports. Still, this information is not necessarily publicly available to other investors.

The second difference is, that hedge funds are free to use nearly every investment strategy including naked short selling and leverage. Leveraging is essentially lending money for the operation executed (e.g. buying amounts of a security), additionally to the capital that is influenced. If a financial firm borrowed exactly as much money for its operations, as it invested own capital, its leverage ratio is one. Although hedge fund's leverage ratios (often up to two) are significantly lower than bank's (at times 15 and higher), there is still a risk attached to this leverage. If the operation goes wrong, not only is the invested money gone, the fund is also in debt for the amount it lent. Although it is disputed, as to what extent this techniques are destabilizing themselves, many other investment vehicles are forbidden to use them.

Lastly, a real difference lies in the individual shares of the investors. A hedge fund will have close to no cash reserves at any given time. On the contrary, as mentioned, hedge funds rather borrow money to multiply the return of their operations. In the case that an investor retreats with his complete share from the fund, it is forced to liquefy a part of its assets in order to pay him off. But because a single investor's share may have several million U.S. dollars of worth, this operation is extremely visible in the markets the fund partakes in. This might induce significant perturbations - even more since investor retreats are likely to correlate with each other.

Official estimations of the U.S. Securities and Exchange Commission (25.07.2013) see the AUM of hedge funds at US$ 4.061 trillion. This figures do not include the extra amount of leveraged money, which is of course also controlled by the hedge funds. Also noteworthy is, that in net asset value terms, only 35% of the hedge funds registered with the CES are U.S. based. This means that the remaining 65% which are active in the U.S. market do not face U.S. regulation; 51% state the Cayman islands as their domicile, which is assumed to be motivated by even less restrictions in that area.

2.3 Regulations and the "shadow market"

As mentioned partly in the preceding paragraphs, there are government-steered attempts to regulate actions of financial institutions into relatively safe perimeters. This results in a complicated net of regulations and laws, minimum ratios, liquidity requirements and other regulatory rules for financial companies. Additionally, these rules vary worldwide, but also within the USA itself. States apply diverse laws regarding similar legal matters. Also the restrictions differ for the type of financial business. While hedge funds face nearly no public documentation obligation or regulation, depository institutions have relatively strict rules.

In the real market, banks are trying to avoid this regulation through a multitude of strategies. One heavily used tactic (that may also serve real organizational purposes) is the splitting of banks into a net of interconnected firms. For activities like the trading of high risk mortgage backed securities, that were mentioned earlier, banks nearly always establish so called "Special Purpose Vehicles". Since they are legally not a bank, this way a lot of regulations do not apply to them anymore. Other firms, especially in the United States, offer services such as lending, that are typically done by a bank, but legally are no bank, thus avoiding regulation. The Financial Stability Board (2011) estimates the worldwide trading volume of this so called "shadow banks" around US$ 60 trillion in 2007, of which circa the half is US-based.

The next chapter will introduce concepts and models from the field of Agent-Based Computational Economics, which are relevant for my concept. Every one of them is incorporated at least once, sometimes transferred to similar problems. There are also combinations of them.

3 Overview of adapted concepts

3.1 Rationality in neoclassical theory

One of the most fundamental assumptions in neoclassical theory is its high reliance on rational choice theory. This theory states that economic subjects act fully rational. It is important to note, that the definition of rationality here is a different one than in common speech. Rationality in this context is rather defined as follows.

Economic subjects have individual preferences which do not contradict themselves. How those preferences evolve is not regarded and for simplification, they remain fixed. If such a subject has to make a decision, it is offered a set of actions. It will then choose between these actions by first applying a personal utility function to each of the actions to determine the expected gain. The subject would also predict all consequences of all actions, calculating their costs. Finally it would choose one of the actions that maximize its personal utility.

The implicit assumptions here are twofold. For one this assumes that there is perfect information available in what a chosen action will result. And secondly, the subject has the capacity (in time and processing ability) to consider every viable choice.

This approach allows for a high rate of formalization of problems which often makes it possible to state economic problems as a calculable optimization problem. Also, if all subjects in the model behave that predictable and formalized, it should be easy to make credible predictions for the future.

3.2 Rationality criticized

But sociologists, psychologists and a rising share of economists start to oppose this assumptions.

"The type of rationality assumed in economics - perfect, logical, deductive rationality [...] demands much of human behavior, much more in fact than it can usually deliver." (Arthur, 1994)

For example behavioral economics suggests that humans and other economic subjects do not act fully rational - neither in the common speech sense nor in the rational choice theory meaning. It is to the day a very controversial question if economic behavior can still be validly **modeled** this way. While the claims it can not are not undisputed (Posner, 1998), one has to admit, that the initial, "strong" rational choice theory[1] has to be altered significantly, to account for seemingly irrational behavior.

And this is being done; for example the model has been enriched by a time-depended utility function, that compensates for the effects of time inconsistency. A lot of other alterations are proposed and used like the introduction of multiple "selves" within a subject, each with different preferences.

"Explaining such behavior in rational-choice terms [...] may require abandoning a tacit assumption of most economic analysts - that the self is a unity - in favor of [...] the person as a locus of different selves." (Posner, 1998)

3.3 Bounded rationality

Another approach to these problems is bounded rationality. This concept, accredited to Herbert A. Simon (1957), deals with the information part of rationality. The main theses behind this approach in contrast to pure rationality are,

- the acquirement of sufficient information for an exhaustive thought process is not effortlessly possible, i.e. has abstract costs

- even with all information available, humans would regularly not be able to process it like described in "strong" rationality due to limitations in their cognitive abilities.

The latter thesis means not only a limited human processing power in comparison to a potentially infinite set of actions. But it may be also intuitive, that for a lot of actions we are simply not able to imagine (deduce) every single consequence.

---

[1]"Strong rationality" is not a widely accepted term in economics. I introduce it to describe rationality in the pure, unaltered definition, as summed up above.

Reacting to this "impediment", Simon (1957) says, humans have developed an alternative strategy. To somehow cope with the complex environment, they apply heuristics to determine costs and consequences (instead of rationally calculating them), causing a simplification of the problems at hand. Eventually this results in only partially rational behavior, where there are irrational or emotional aspects in the decision process.

3.4 Application of bounded rationality to agent-based models

3.4.1 Wide variety of bounded rationality aspects

When designing multi-agent based computational economics models, the idea of bounded rationality may be incorporated in a multitude of ways. Depending on the nature of the model, the designer has to consider models from various other scientific disciplines. Generally, there are three approaches available. The first one is to limit the information available to the agent via an implicit model of its perception. The second is, to build explicit representations of information costs. The last possibility deals less with the perception, than with the processing aspect of decision making.

3.4.2 Modeling (positive) information costs for agents

Implicit models, or "How to be human"

An explicit model restricts the availability of information, often according to real world physics. Imagine for example, a model of individual humans maundering over a classical farmer's market or through the aisles of a supermarket. It could prove interesting, to employ models from cognition theory, simple "physics" models, image-processing methods, or any other arbitrary combination of theories, to imitate human environment perception. This way the positive cost of gathering information is modeled, in the form, that an agent has to look and walk around the environment to acquire it. Of course this is not only true for economic models, but for nearly every spatially explicit multi-agent simulation that holds "human" agents. Limited line of sight as a consequence of a smoky environment in a burning building is just another example of the application of this idea.

The mentioned examples are all implicitly modeling the abstract costs of gathering information. They are an intuitive approach, since they try to replicate real-life experiences nearly every human should have had in his life. It is therefore not surprising, that the general idea of positive information costs is widely accepted in economic theory. But in different families of ABMs, and in economics this is quite common, spatial orientation and an explicit, computable depiction of a material environment are not of interest. If you build e.g. a stock trading simulation[2], the physical environment should play a minor role.

Explicit models of information cost (Information market)

Nevertheless, a modeler might be interested in not only limiting the individual information of an agent, thus adding heterogeneity to his model, but making information potentially available to the agent, if it pays enough "attention". In this case, it may be required to explicitly model positive information cost. This as well is common practice in economic theory.

Unfortunately, I was not able to find any scientific information on models of explicit positive information costs in an ABM context. One concept could be that of an "information market". Again, there is not yet an accepted definition for the term "information market". Different source define it conflictingly (for example compare Hanson (2003) with Wikipedia Foundation (2013)). However, the term (and related concepts, like trading or costs of information) are used quite often. A possible instance of that concept, as I use it in my simulation model, is explained in the section information market.

Cognition and decision process models

Overview of decision process modeling approaches So far we have only dealt with how information is perceived. What amount comes when, and in which quality to the agent's knowledge? This is more about the first thesis of bounded rationality. But in a multi-agent based model, no matter how the perception is modeled, there must always be a "mind". Without independently acting agents, there is no agent-based simulation. The second thesis revolves more around this topic.

From a computer science point of view, we can resort to two main categories of answers for this problem. Either we have available (or develop) a fully rational model of the decision process. Something like that is, to say the least, ambitious. Or we try to somehow approximate the human cognition process.

---

[2]A modern, computer-based stock market. In an environment, where traders have to physically get in contact with others in order to trade, a spatially explicit simulation model might actually pose interesting research questions.

Numerical optimization and learning   One way of this approximation would be, to apply some kind of optimization technique. One of the most often used in computational economics is genetic algorithms (LeBaron, 2006). But of course there are many others: numerical algorithms, temporal difference learning, artificial neural networks, searching, to name some. In computer science, those approaches, each with their pros and cons, are widely known and well-defined.

But there are three reasons why I do not want to focus on applying one of them. The first one is simply: When I quote the names, a rough plan already exists on how to do it. Though examining the results would also be interesting, the general idea is not really new; I would rather like to walk off the beaten track. The second reason goes somewhat along Occam's razor: If at least one of the mentioned techniques works (i.e. produces credible results), that is of course a good thing. But when describing a model, applying complex algorithms for such a central part is (at least something) like putting a "black-box" at that spot. It is worth at least some effort to look for simpler descriptions. Last, but not least: the main idea of bounded rationality is, that humans often do *not* make optimal decisions. So, even if one manages to successfully apply an optimization technique, there is a risk of not modeling how humans *do* behave, but rather how they *should*.

Hence, in the next section I focus more on the alternative approach: Models that focus less on "automatic" optimization but on heuristics and other simple concepts.

3.5 Heterogeneous (Expectations) Agent Models (HAM)

3.5.1 Basic idea

In 1994, the American Economic Review released a paper by W. Brian Arthur called "Inductive Reasoning and Bounded Rationality" (Arthur, 1994). In this paper he pondered exactly the question of how to model bounded rationality. Referring to modern psychology, he states, that humans are perform moderately at deductive thinking and that   *"... we make only moderate use of it."* (Arthur, 1994).

The concept he then introduces, is analogous to the process that psychology implies. Humans seem to mostly prefer inductive reasoning above deductive processes, especially in complicated or ill-defined circumstances. He proposes a model that tries to imitate the process in the human cognition.

Each agent carries a set of personal models, heuristics (also called predictors) with which it explains its world. There is always an "active" or preferred model of explanation [3]. Based on the preferred heuristic, the agent makes assumptions on how the environment will react to its action. The agent then chooses its action according to the preferred predictor(s). Generally, the active heuristic differs among the agents. Hence the name heterogeneous expectations model. While the agent makes new experiences it evaluates the performance of its predictor. If the active heuristic performs badly repeatedly, the agent will change its active heuristic. Normally the new heuristic will be one of the better performing; mostly the best.

This model is illustrated with the example of a bar, that a set of agents would potentially like to visit. In the example there are 100 agents. However they only decide to go there, if they expect the number of guests to be under 60.

The set of heuristics for the agents consists of the following ones

- the same as last week

- 100 - (nr. of visitors last week)

- (rounded) average of the last four weeks

- the trend in the last 8 weeks, bounded by 0,100

- the same as 2 weeks ago

- the same as 5 weeks ago

This list could of course be easily extended further. All agents share the same set of heuristics, but the initially favored one is distributed randomly. You may notice, that it did not risk the results much, if there were inefficient or unreasonable heuristics in the set. Since the agents choose a good performing one most of the time, and switch only to other well performing, bad ones are simply ignored.

When running this setting for 100 weeks, the agents interestingly manage to form a pattern, where the number of attendants oscillates closely around the mark of the mentioned 60%. The population remains in a state where around 60% of agents expect the number to be less than

---

[3]It is also possible to imagine the model with a set of active heuristics, but for simplicity's sake this was in the paper reduced to one. Interestingly, psychology suggests, that humans actually tend to prefer exactly one hypothesis at any time.

60 and 40% expect more. But which agent is in which group changes every week. This is also true for the preferred predictors. There is none that works all the time, but instead, the agents change their believes continuously and so, though nearly everything else changes, the 60/40 pattern persists.

3.5.2 Adaptation and generalization

The very core of this model was further discussed, analyzed and refined in the following years (see e.g. Arthur *et al.* (30.11.1996), LeBaron (2006), Hommes (2006b), Hommes (2006a), and many more). Laboratory studies were conducted to compare and verify the experiment's results more realistically (Anufriev & Hommes, 2012). The remarkable property of certain configurations of this model is that, in contrast to homogeneous agent models, they *"were able to match moments of different financial variables and generate several "stylized facts" of financial markets, such as excess volatility, volatility clustering, and fat tails of the return distribution."* (Anufriev & Hommes, 2012).

Since my main interest in financial model simulation is on the dynamics that lead to bubble formation and the following collapses, I find this very important to note. Several models that included the heuristics switching mechanism as described at the start of the chapter are the only [4] ones capable of explaining many phenomena at once, that for a long time puzzled economists. Simply when influencing the initial distribution of preferred heuristics or agent's willingness to switch the heuristics, the models exhibit relevant patterns. Among them a stable attraction to an equilibrium price *as well as* excess volatility and bubble formation (followed by bursts). And all that completely out of the model, without external intervention.

But those mentioned models all focus on financial markets that are more or less stylized versions of something like a stock market. In the focus are single, independent traders. But how could this concept be transferred to a wider area, that (in the best case) deals with all activities in that banks engage nowadays? The next chapter introduces a model that is a step towards a way of modeling this.

---

[4]This includes models with fixed sets of focal ("gut reaction") heuristics as well as dynamic heuristics development mechanisms such as genetic algorithms or neural nets.

3.6 Movement within a strategy hypercube as a model for banking strategy

3.6.1 Model description

When imagining the decisions that a bank management faces it may be easy to see, that a crucial aspect in nearly every decision is the expectation of future developments. But even to define a bank's current (or targeted) strategic position in a compact way is not easy. "Our credit customer distribution leans too much towards risky investments" may be comprehensible to humans, but we need a model that is somehow expressible in computer terms and covers not only one aspect but the bank's status as a whole.

Robertson (2003) builds a model that - at least partially - addresses this topic. After explaining previous work on strategic dimensions, he names a few examples that, according to this work, could be relevant in an agent-based model. A dimension in this context could be something like the bank's number of products or a measurement for their differentiation. His focus, in contrast to the referred literature, is the (non-linear) dynamic of bank's movements within these dimensions. For the purpose of examining the resulting characteristics, he models a very basic and stylized bank market.

For the exact details I refer to the paper, but the concept I want to emphasize is the "strategy hypercube", which the model's agents (banks as well as customers) populate. The author designs it in a quite intuitive way. It derives from the mathematical definition of an n-dimensional space. Each of the dimensions D_{0-n} represents a range of values, that are model-relevant and represent strategically important dimensions that a bank may have a position in. A good example could be a credit card debt interest rate. The exact position of a bank can then formally be described as a tuple of the form $(v_1 \in D_1, v_2 \in D_2, ..., v_n \in D_n)$. The elements of the dimensions can be more or less arbitrary, but generally they would be subsets of $\mathbb{N}$ or $\mathbb{R}$. Since those subsets are almost always bounded, he refers to the resulting space as a "strategy hypercube" as opposed to "strategy n -space". The concrete strategy of any bank is then defined as its movement pattern through this strategy hypercube.

There is a wide variety of possible patterns of this movement. In the model described, the author opted for a pre-determined set of heuristics, namely "stay still", "follow the lead bank" or "customer orientation" [5]. Unfortunately it was not explicitly stated, if the agents also switch between the heuristics like in the HAM model. The way, the results are presented, indicates that the banks hold on to a strategies throughout one simulation run. There were two "environments" defined, one where the customers stood still, and another "turbulent environment", where customers were random walking through the space.

3.6.2 Discussion

The definition of this model allows easy calculations to determine, say, the distance between two competitors. It is a very elegant way to describe a bank's position and its strategy. The processing aspect was not even mentioned, but the definition of the model would allow for every approach I mentioned earlier. Next to a fully rational solution for the bank's agents, bounded rationality can be applied here as well. As Robertson also suggests, one could decide to greatly enhance the model's complexity by introducing more (realistic) dimensions or using learning algorithms instead of pre-defined heuristics. But even in this simple configuration, the model showed interesting, non-linear behavior.

A drawback of this model lies in the definition of the dimensions. In a nontrivial application, a value of a banking strategy dimension is often very complex in itself. Consider for example a distribution of loan contracts over a heterogeneous group of customers in terms of credit risk. Transforming such higher dimensional constructs to a 1-dimensional representation inevitably sacrifices accuracy. Closely related to this is, that the number of concrete dimensions tends to increase rapidly in this transformation process. This results in a very complex solution space, that may get increasingly difficult to optimize even with efficient techniques. The modeler is forced to find a trade-off between the number of dimensions and the accuracy of the described dimensions.

---

[5] Here, the bank would try staying at its customer's "center of mass"

4 Simulation model

4.1 Considerations, exclusions, design principles

This chapter describes the simulation model I developed. First the model's purpose and focus, my resulting fundamental design decisions, (among them the deliberate exclusion of certain aspects) are pointed out. Then, the main parts describe each model element in detail.

4.1.1 Purpose of the model and incorporated ACE models

The main purpose of this model is to raise the understanding of the dynamics and (in the optimal case) help testing means for reducing the probability and magnitude of market-wide crashes in the financial sector. To get closer to reality, the model is more detailed than the relatively abstract and stylized models from chapter three. Due to their ability to generate many desired real-world features, most importantly endogenous shocks, it tries to adopt their main ideas. On the other hand, it is still a model, so it should not include *every* detail of the real market. Due to f the original topic's complexity, this is not an easy task.

Because of their promising results, the models from chapter three and bounded rationality in general are often included. While the concept tries to resemble imperfect decision processes, explicit models of human's feelings are generally avoided. Modeling human feelings and their impact on decisions (for every agent model in the concept) is a whole research field for itself, even more so in computer models. Representing it everywhere would exceed the extent of my thesis.

4.1.2 The role of real market data

As the reader might have noticed, I have cited many sources for statistical data, especially in the economic basics chapter. As far as it is feasible, I tried to incorporate this data into every aspect of the model, to reach a higher degree of relevance for reality. In some cases, model elements just apply historical data to the simulation as a function of time. In other cases, the data could be used for model initialization (for example the account balances of private credit customers). This data is crucial for verification, calibration and validation as well. And finally, since the model contains a lot of original research, sometimes statistics were examined, just to get a general idea of the aspect in question.

Unfortunately, the usefulness and availability of data in different subjects is very hetero-geneous depending on the model's aspects. Macro economical figures have a good chance of being well documented and fairly easy to access, although even here there are problems. Many sources demand money for data older than 5 years. Others do not even have it. The real problems start with micro economics. As far as I can see, there is no micro data available for many relevant model aspects. This made it really cumbersome or even impossible, to develop an idea for each relevant sub-model. Still, a lot of the macro data can be used to derive initial conditions of the model or validate its outputs.

4.2 Overview of the model

4.2.1 Model elements

Figure 4.1 shows an overview of the model. An arrow indicates that the source entity influences the target element in any way. On the top level, the model consists of fear agent types, the asset market and the federal reserve system. Agents are active in banks and hedge funds interacting with each other and two different types of loan customers. Banks interact with nearly every entity in the model. They borrow money to each other, to hedge funds or to non-financial loan customers. Hedge funds and banks also partake at the offering and buying of assets on the asset market. The interaction between banks and loan customers has the general form of a customer asking banks for a loan, the bank "considering" that request and either accepting the contract or not. The same is of course true for financial sector customers. If the loan is not rejected, the customer starts paying interest according to his individual model. The Federal Reserve System influences most processes by setting economic parameters, offering credit to commercial banks and open market operations via the asset market. The parameters either affect the profitability of deals, or have the character of hard restrictions, like the minimum reserve rate.

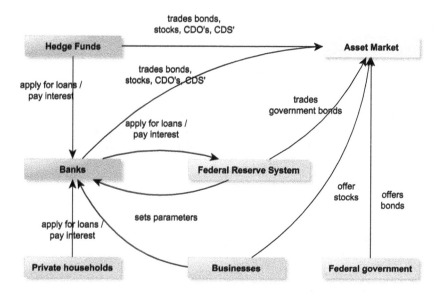

Figure 4.1: general overview

The one element that is not shown in the overview, to keep the picture well-arranged, is an information market. It is an explicit model of the cost of acquiring information as mentioned in chapter three. Nearly all model elements produce and "consume" information.

4.2.2 Categorization of credit types

All the possible credit types in reality are categorized into one of the following categories (see figure 4.2.2), which the model differentiates. In the real world, there are even more forms. The model tries to consider the various types of credit, while at the same time represent some kind of abstraction.

4.2.3 Model execution

The whole model is calculated in synchronous, global steps, however some sub-systems may go through several internal cycles to calculate one global step. This structure accounts for the

securitized	non-securitized
mortgage loans	other private loans
corporate loans	public loans
purchasing credits	

Figure 4.2: categorization of loans

varying dynamics of the modeled real-world subsystems. While some mechanisms at work are being sped up as fast as technically feasible in the real world (i.e. high frequency stock trading), others (Federal Reserve System) remain relatively slow in comparison, with action times measured in months.

The following sections describe all elements and their interactions in detail.

4.3 The bank agent

4.3.1 Banking agent systems' structure

The bank's agent is actually an "agent system", that consists of three parts, integrated with each other. They describe the bank's different channels of interaction and "level of consciousness". The internal structure mimics real-world corporate structures, but is kept simple to avoid going into the details too much. Modularizing the bank into smaller sub-agents brings the known advantages, like separation of concerns and reduced complexity in the single parts. But the most important reason this is done here is, that this way the different models for the parts of the behavior are easily interchangeable, thus allowing for more flexibility in experiments with different model parts.

If the Management part is considered to be the bank's "brain", then the Loan Retailing and Investment Banking agents are more like its "hands". They interact directly with the outside (i.e. customers or asset market). The management agent steers how they do it. Still, many parts are full agents, each with their own cycle of perception, decision making, interaction. In many other agent models, there is also an interpretation stage in the

Figure 4.3: the bank agent's internal structure

cycle, that alters the perception before the
decision making. With the exception of the management agent, this step is either left out or
rudimentary as opposed to explicitly defined in the model.

4.3.2 Management agent

Overview

The management agent's model represents the strategic decision level of a bank. It is responsible for setting the bank's general market approach. Its model draws extensively on the concepts of bounded rationality and the strategy-hypercube model explained in the chapter Overview of adapted concepts.

This is applied here in three ways. For one the management agent processes very little information. The only information that is used in the decision process are a limited number of past profits the bank made and the corresponding strategies, that were used to realize them. By ignoring a lot of theoretically available information, to concentrate on one seemingly important aspect, I try to form an analogy to the human mind applying very strict information filtering.

Secondly, similar to the Heterogeneous Agent Model (HAM) (Hommes, 2006b), the management agent's decision process revolves around sets of available, heuristically formed expectations of the action option's consequences. The model is more complex, but I try to maintain the main notion of the original theory.

The third model element that weakens full rationality is that each bank management has an abstract risk perception value that determines its tendency to opt for actions commonly considered as risky. This risk perception value is not static; it is influenced by the agent's "experiences". The intention behind this element is to emulate the cyclic risk taking behavior resulting from self-reinforcing patterns in humans which is used in several disciplines like psychology and even computer science (see temporal difference learning).

The way of representing the banks' strategy options in my model is greatly influenced by the strategy-hypercube model from Robertson (2003). However, it is not a direct copy. The two main differences are, that it is more detailed than the original one, in terms of available dimensions, strategies and strategy switching. Additionally, the execution of selected strategies is more sophisticated than in the original. The next sections will explain these differences in detail, starting with the employed dimensions that comprise the strategy hypercube.

Determination of the hyper-cube's dimensions

debt-to-equity-ratio One of the first parameters, that a bank management can use to steer its risk management, is its targeted debt-to-equity ratio. Comparison of this values is non-trivial, because the regulations for calculating the ratio differ not only from country to country, but even between different companies. Of particular interest are questions like: What is considered capital and what is an asset? How to account for the fact that assets may have varying values when one is trying to monetize them in an emergency situation? Especially the last question is with regards to the financial crisis of greatest interest. Within this thesis I will use the following definition.

$$\textit{debt-to-equity ratio} = \frac{\textit{tier 1 capital}}{\textit{balance sheet total}}$$

For the model, this number will be a non-discrete real number $0 < ratio \leq 1$.

minimum reserve rate Although the lowest allowed value is dictated by the central bank (i.e. the Federal Reserve System), banks can always choose to exceed the minimum reserve rate. This becomes especially interesting, if the interest paid on excess reserves comes close to or is higher than the interest a bank can earn with other investments. It also tends to happen in times where banks are uncertain about their mutual credibility (Die Zeit, 2011-11-22).

dividends and bonuses It is also intuitively important for the management, to decide what happens with the earnings from its different businesses. The earnings can be distributed among three different options. It can either add them to the bank's balance, pay dividends to share holders, or pay bonuses to its employees. In practice, mixtures of all three options can be observed. The next two dimensions influence this distribution for a simulated bank. The dimension $s_{dividend}$ sets what part of the bank's earnings is distributed as dividend to share holders, respectively, the s_{bonus} is responsible for bonus payments to the management. The part that raises the bank's capital is what remains after the other shares are subtracted. The shares can be any positive integer number, including zero and are to be read as

$$\frac{1}{share}$$

of the earnings.

credit interest rates   Another credit related value that is obviously important to influence is the interest rate i for the different credit types.

While values of this parameters could theoretically be anything within $\mathbb{Z}$, real and simulated values should be in the range $0 \geq i \leq 10$.

credit-risk-distributions   Each and every form of investment or loan carries an inherent risk attached, that influences its fundamental value. Thus it is of vital importance for a bank management, to prevent risks from accumulating to a magnitude that endangers the institution as a whole. Then again, riskier investments also tend to promise higher interest. So to compete with other institutions (and to increase its own salary, since that is bound directly to the bank's earnings) the management is interested in taking at least some risk. Hence, a set of parameters that are intuitively important for a bank to control are the risk distributions for its investment and loan businesses.

The one-dimensional representations of all credit segment's risk distributions follow the same pattern. It adopts the banking procedure that divides (potential) loan customers into "prime" and "subprime" groups. The dimensions specify the share of subprime customers for the corresponding credit type. The rest of are, accordingly, in the prime segment. The possible values of this dimensions are a real number $0 \geq subprime - ratio \leq 1$. As there are 5 different credit types in the model, there are 5 dimensions for their risk distributions.

Borders between prime and subprime   Directly related to the prime versus subprime categorization of potential credit customers is the exact border between prime and subprime customers. The next dimensions derive from that. The model assumes, that the creditors are able to relatively precisely determine the default risk for their customers. Each dimension sets the bank's border between prime and subprime customers for the corresponding credit type. The dimensions appoint where the range of annual default risk, starting at 0, ends in which customers are assumed to be prime. Possible values for the prime border b are all real numbers in the range $0 \geq b \leq 100$.

Available strategies and their application

In this section, the available strategies and the decision process model that chooses one are discussed. The idea is, to retain the structure of the HAM model, but make it applicable to

Name	min.	max.	Description
r_{de}	0	1	debt-to-equity-ratio
$r_{reserve}$	0	100	rate of reserve at central bank
$s_{dividend}$	0	∞	$\frac{1}{s_{dividend}}$ of bank's earnings are paid as dividends
s_{bonus}	0	∞	$\frac{1}{s_{bonus}}$ of bank's earnings are paid as bonuses
$i_{mortgage}$	0	1	mortgage loan interest rate
$d_{mortgage}$	0	1	mortgage risk distribution
$b_{mortgage}$	0	100	(inclusive) prime border for mortgage customers
$i_{corporate}$	0	1	corporate loan interest rate
$d_{corporate}$	0	1	corporate loan risk distribution
$b_{corporate}$	0	100	(inclusive) prime border for corporate customers
$i_{purchase}$	0	1	purchasing credit interest rate
$d_{purchase}$	0	1	purchasing credit risk distribution
$b_{purchase}$	0	100	(inclusive) prime border for purchasing credit
$i_{private}$	0	1	other private loan interest rate
$d_{private}$	0	1	risk distribution for other private loans
$b_{private}$	0	100	(inclusive) prime border for other private loan customers
i_{public}	0	1	public loan interest rate
d_{public}	0	1	public credit risk distribution
b_{public}	0	100	(inclusive) prime border for public customers

Figure 4.4: overview of strategy hyper-cube dimensions

the strategy hypercube model at the same time. Similar to the original strategy hypercube model, the agent can choose from a set of available options to steer through the strategy space. But there are also some differences between the models. For instance, the options are not heuristics but strategies.

A strategy is defined here as a set $S = \{(d, v) | d$ is a strategy hypercube dimension $\wedge v \in \{\triangle, \triangledown\} \wedge \forall (d', v') \in S : d \neq d'\}$. Or in natural language, a (unique) selection of strategy hypercube dimensions, with which a value change in the direction increase value or decrease dimension are associated. A special case of this is the empty strategy $S = \varnothing$ which simply means change nothing, stay still. Those strategies can still be compared to heuristics for they both try to implement a notion of what seems to be "a good idea". The actual set of available strategies and its creation will be discussed later in this section. First, the process that determines if and how strategies are adopted is explained.

The decision process

Maybe the most profound difference to the original strategy hypercube is that, influenced by the HAM model, the management agent switches between the available strategies throughout a simulation run.

The management agent is assumed to try to maximize its short-term profit. As long as its income increases, at least slightly, it will stay at its exact position. If the income stagnates on the same level repeatedly, this will result in linearly declining satisfaction. If the income development is even downwards, the agent will be exponentially unsatisfied. When the satisfaction level crosses a given threshold, the agent is discontent. In this status it will change its strategy from "stay still" to one that changes the target position. If the profits start to increase again, the satisfaction (and thus the status) reset to a neutral level, from which the satisfaction rises back again.

Unfortunately, strategies do not directly produce a measurable value for the future, which could then be used to measure its performance by comparing the prognosticated value with the realized one. As a consequence, it is not possible to switch to the "best" strategy when the current one fails repeatedly, because it is not certain, which one is the best.

To address this problem, the bank management agent's decision process chooses not by comparing prognosticated values to realized ones but by "remembering" past experiences with

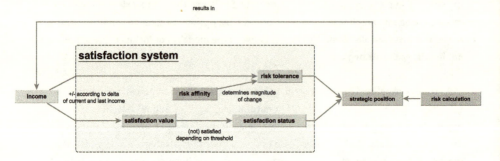

Figure 4.5: management agent's internal structure

strategies. Thus, strategies - at least indirectly - have a comparable performance measure, that allows for a selection. Due to the dynamic nature of the agent's environment, its assumptions about the quality of strategies may be outdated. But if that is the case, negative experiences are going to occur while pursuing it, resulting in a declining performance measure for the strategy, eventually causing another one to appear more attractive.

Parallel to this relatively rational process, there is an "irrational" system that influences the agent's decisions. Every management agent has a risk tolerance and a risk affinity. An agent's risk affinity can be considered a character trait and does not change during a simulation run. In contrast to that, the risk tolerance has a dynamic attached to it. Strategic decisions have abstract costs, that can be positive or negative. This cost is charged against the agent's risk tolerance every time it chooses to pursue any given strategy. For example, decreasing the debt-to-equity ratio will always have positive[1] risk costs, resulting in a higher risk tolerance value. In contrast, other strategies might have negative risk costs, as for example raising a d or b dimension allows for a bigger customer base but also introduces more risk in the credit departments.

So when an agent decides to try another strategy, the selection of possible strategies neglects those that bare a risk, which the management is not willing to afford at the moment. However, if a management chooses (or sticks to) a strategy that has negative costs and that results in positive income developments, its risk tolerance "account" receives a slightly greater

---

[1]Since it makes the bank more prone against risks, while at the same time reducing profit opportunities, especially because of a reduced leverage effect.

balance than it had before choosing this option.

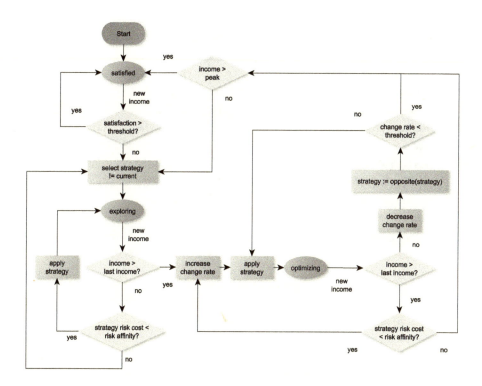

Figure 4.6: management agent's decision process cycle

Strategy derivation The strategies made available to the agent try to give a lot of freedom. The stay still and follow the leader strategies are taken from the original model (Robertson, 2003), but are also quite intuitive. Each value can also be separately increased and decreased, to allow for "fine tuning" of any dimension's target and to lower the effect of valid, (potentially) missing strategies. The remaining ones were composed by me. They derive from observation of real world data changes, as well as common sense of what may seem viable. The pattern, that for every strategy there is also the exact opposite, is used through the entire list.

Name	Formally
Stay still	∅
Follow the leader	dynamic, dependent on leader position
Backpedal	Return to a former position
Increase one of the single values	$\{(d, \triangle)\}$ [2]
Decrease one of the single values	$\{(d, \triangledown)\}$
Increased bonuses by leverage	$\{(r_{de}, \triangledown), (s_{bonus}, \triangle)\}$
Reduce bonuses and leverage	$\{(r_{de}, \triangle), (s_{bonus}, \triangledown)\}$
Distribute profit	$\{(s_{dividend}, \triangle), (s_{bonus}, \triangle)\}$
Save more profit	$\{(s_{dividend}, \triangledown), (s_{bonus}, \triangledown)\}$
Less but riskier subprime customers	$\{(b_x, \triangle)(d_x, \triangledown)\}$ [3]
More but less risky subprime customers	$\{(b_x, \triangledown), (d_x, \triangle)\}$
Increase general credit risk	$\{(b_x, \triangle), (d_x, \triangle)\}$
Decrease general credit risk	$\{(b_x, \triangledown), (d_x, \triangledown)\}$
Increase general credit risk w. higher interest	$\{(b_x, \triangle), (d_x, \triangle), (i_x, \triangle)\}$
Decrease general credit risk w. lower interest	$\{(b_x, \triangledown), (d_x, \triangledown), (i_x, \triangledown)\}$

Figure 4.7: available strategies

Application of strategies After the management has set its desired position, the position's target values influence the other bank agents in their decisions. It is important to notice, that the bank management's decisions can often not be directly realized. While buying and selling assets is (relatively) easy, credit contracts can generally not be canceled very fast. Instead, the other agents will try to push the actual values in the direction of the target in new deals.

4.3.3 Loan retailing

The loan retailer is responsible for making contracts with potential credit customers. In contrast to other parts of the simulation it is not really an autonomously acting agent. Instead, it is more a conceptual segment of the bank agent. Nonetheless it makes decisions about incoming credit applications and the resulting customer based risks. In general, it tries to match the targets set by the bank management.

Processing applications for the several branches of credit has overall the same form: acquire as many customers as possible, asses their default risks, calculate if the resulting credit risk seems reasonable, and offer a contract. However, risk calculation is a difficult task. This holds true for default risk assessment, as well as overall credit risk that also has to assume correctness and relies on the default risk values. What complicates the matter even further are the several forms of credit.

4.3.4 Investment banking

The investment banking segment houses multiple (tens of) individual trading agents. Each agent manages an own portfolio of (for simplification exactly) 25 securities and a personal budget. Also, there is no separate logic for managing the "employees" of the investment banking department. Their number and identity stay the same over one simulation run, completely unaffected by their performance. The investment banking components of the model calculate 48 simulation steps per global simulation step and trading agent. This is to imitate a frequency of one transaction opportunity every ten minutes of an 8 hour work day. The execution order is pseudo-randomized over all individual investment banking agents to avoid a situation, were a particular agent or firm has advantages because it gets to act first unfairly often.

The model of a trading agent is built around an adapted heterogeneous expectations agent as described in chapter three. Depending on with which version of HAM one compares, there are three differences. One agent does not only trade one or two abstract assets as in the other models, but 25. The heuristics set does not change at runtime, and the trading agents are all technical traders.

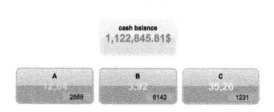

Figure 4.8: exemplary portfolio

Arthur et al. (30.11.1996) uses an approach, where the agents can form their expectations function through a genetic algorithm. In that approach, the agents can generate fundamental functions, or technical trading ones, or mixtures of both themselves. Also, the agents can favor multiple expectation functions. It is an interesting concept, but a reasonably elaborate model for that approach within this simulation model would cost a lot of time. Even more since in contrast to the stochastically calculated, "correct" fundamental value in (e.g.) Arthur *et al.* (30.11.1996), this model has no intrinsic definition of the fundamental value. So there would be a need to not only build a model for the generation of expectations functions, but also a model for the fundamental values. Hence, this step is left out for the present. I choose a more static approach similar to that in Arthur (1994). It should be no problem to include a more complex version later.

Name	Abbrev.	Formally
Adaptive heuristic[1]	ADA	$p^e_{g,t+1} = 0.65p_{t-1} + 0.35p^e_{1,t}$
Weak trend-following rule[1]	WTR	$p^e_{g,t+1} = p_{t-1} + 0.4(p_{t-1} - p_{t-2})$
Strong trend-following rule[1]	STR	$p^e_{g,t+1} = p_{t-1} + 1.3(p_{t-1} - p_{t-2})$
Anchoring and adjustment rule with learning anchor[1]	LAA	$p^e_{g,t+1} = 0.5(p^{av}_{t-1} + p_{t-1}) + (p_{t-1} - p_{t-2})$
Same as last rule[2]	SAL	$p^e_{g,t+1} = p_{g,t-1}$
Same as 1 week ago rule[2]	SA1W	$p^e_{g,t+1} = p_{g,t-7\times48}$
Same as 2 week ago rule[2]	SA2W	$p^e_{g,t+1} = p_{g,t-7\times48}$
1 hour trend rule	1HTR	$p^e_{g,t+1} =$ extrapolation of $\sum_{j=t-5\times6}^{t-1} p_{g,j}$ with least squares trend
5 day trend rule	5DTR	$p^e_{g,t+1} =$ extrapolation of $\sum_{j=t-5\times8\times6}^{t-1} p_{g,j}$ with least squares trend

Figure 4.9: trading agent heuristics set

Static in this context means that the expectations function set does not change at runtime. And as in Anufriev & Hommes (2012) or Arthur (1994), the agents have only one "active" expectation function, on which they rely for actual forecasting. The list of the available heuristics can be seen in 4.3.4. Most of them are gathered from the ones described in Anufriev & Hommes (2012) and Arthur (1994) [4]. The "2" rules might be adjusted slightly to fit this simulation model, but are still inspired by the source.

The agent guesses at step t in time, for every good g, the expected price in the next step ($p^e_{g,t+1}$). Note that the "AA" rule is missing, since it refers to a fundamental price. The $p^{av}_{t-1} = \frac{1}{t}\sum_{j=0}^{t-1} p_{g,j}$ denotes a sample average of past prices, that is considered to provide a

---

[4]Rules from the first source are marked with [1], the ones from the second source with [2]

proxy for the fundamental price (Anufriev & Hommes, 2012). The constant factors in the "1" rules originate from empirical data and are explained in the original source. The integer factors in the "2"-rules derive from the assumptions about calculation steps in the beginning of this subsection. If no data back to the designated point is available, which is the case at simulation start, the row of data points is shortened. At a later point, it would be more accurate to use correct, historic data, if it is available.

As seen in chapter three, the HAM model uses one "active" heuristic to estimate the security's future value and switches to a better one, if the active heuristic significantly fails to predict the future. In the trading agent, this whole process is done per security. This implies, that a trading agent may as well have completely different heuristics to predict the development of each security at any point in time.

4.4 Hedge funds

Figure 4.10: the hedge fund agent's structure

For a long time I intended to leave out this model part, since the model is already relatively big. But the more research I did for this thesis, the more it seemed like (1) the biggest american banks behave like hedge funds, if they can, and (2) there are strong hints, that the interaction of both is very important for today's financial sector in the USA. For example there is the mere volume of money, hedge funds can move in a short amount of time.

Since the bank agent was built modular and the bank agent already has an "investment banking" module, which in reality trades assets, it can be configured without a loan retailer and the rest of the logic remains the same. It also works very similar to the bank agents - with the difference, that the parameters for credit assignment are ignored. To my knowledge, hedge funds grant credit rarely at maximum.

4.5 The asset market

The asset market is the part of the concept that allows for most interaction within the financial sector. It is a combination of various real world markets. Offers include stocks, collateralized debt obligations, credit default swaps, government securities and commodities like gold and silver. The market model works similar to the mechanism in stock trading, but with some abstractions. The most important one is, that everything is traded at this market. There is no differentiation in any way between any of the traded assets. Also, making transactions or partaking at the market at all does not produce costs.

The market itself works like a simplified version of real stock market trading systems. Potential sellers can offer predefined quantities of an asset at a minimum price. That offer is called an ask. Buyers interested in the offered assets can place bids, which also comprise of a quantity of an asset at a maximum price. The market system then tries to match bids and asks always when a new one comes in. When the ask price is lower than a compatible bid price (which should be the common case) and the ask price is used to complete the transaction, sellers have a systematic disadvantage. The other way around, when using the bid price, the buyers are always aggrieved. Until finishing this thesis I found no reliable source for information on how real stock trading systems deal with this problem. To reduce this bias, the market system here sets the price for any successful transaction at $askprice + \frac{bid\ price - ask\ price}{2}$. Assuming that most market participants sell approximately as much assets as they buy, this should reduce the bias to a tolerable level.

4.6 Loan customer types

This part describes the different types of potential customers that apply for loans at banks and their model. Generally, there are three different types of customers: private households, companies and public households. Generally, the model does not consider customers that do not apply for credits. Of interest are only individuals or institutions that are interested in any form of credit.

Interconnections between the different credit branches or its participants are not part of the model. I would have been very interested to include a lot more of detail especially in this part. There are many aspects that could greatly influence results. Examples are regional relations, the effects of evictions on house prices in the neighborhood or the impact of changing employment rates on the ability of private households to meet credit payments. However, the nature of those relations is as controversial as many other of my topics and forms own fields of study. Hence, to keep the thesis within the time frame, the connections are not included and the customer models themselves are relatively abstract.

4.6.1 Private households

Private households are interested in two kinds of bank loans. The first ones are related to mortgages with medium volumes and relatively long durations. The second one are integrated in the category "other private loans". This includes consumer credits as well as credit card debt, or personal credit lines for bank accounts which typically feature low volumes and very short durations [5].

One private household agents may apply for both mortgages and other private credits at the same time. For the purpose of simplification, all agents are expected to have exactly one account at any of the given banks.

The agents have four (at the moment) immutable properties, a saving rate r, a job security factor s, its value at the job market v and its mobility (m). The saving rate is defined as an (absolute) monthly amount of money that the household saves up for credit payments in bad times. The job security factor determines the probability, with which the household will have at least one employed member next month who is able to generate income. The value of v denotes the chance of the household to regain a position with regular income again for the next month if it is unemployed at the moment. Finally, m is the monthly chance that a household will consider switching its bank.

In times where there is income, the household carries out credit payments and deposits savings at its bank according to r. If there is no income, payments are met using the savings. Only if there is no income and no savings left, the agent does not pay. Also it is calculated by chance if the income situation persists for the next month using s. Analogously, if the household has no income at the time, it gets back into regular employment with a chance of $1 : v$. Always when

---

[5] In reality, account credit lines and credit-card debt tend to get paid off only after months and years. But technically, this is because of contracts with a common length of 30 days which are just automatically renewed. Banks and credit card companies correspondingly normally do not guarantee instauration of those contracts, reserving the right to reject it on a monthly basis.

```
balance ← 1.5r // a realistic amount previous savings
hasIncome ← {true|false} // realistic distribution of employment
while // simulation running do
    if hasIncome then
        // pay off rate
        balance ← balance + r
        if randomDouble() > s then
            hasIncome ← false
        end if
    else
        if balance > creditPayment then
            // pay off rate
            balance ← balance − creditPayment
        end if
        if randomDouble() < v then
            hasIncome ← true
            searchForBetterBank()
        end if
    end if
end while
```

Figure 4.11: one private customers algorithm

its situation changes from no income to income [6] and also with a chance of $1 : m$ every month, the agent looks for a potentially better bank. So for each month the agent runs through a non-deterministic process that is directly influenced by its values as shown in this pseudo code.

The search for a better bank works mostly rational. The available offerings for the products the household uses, are sorted in ascending order with regards to the interest paid. If the top one is cheaper than what the household has, then it switches to the bank with that offer. But to make the switching behavior more realistic, this process is not completely rational. Instead of searching within all available banks, the household only uses a list of five banks. The chance of a bank to be on this list is directly proportional to its market share in percent. It should be safe to assume that these restrictions to a perfect search resemble more realistic conditions. No normal household has the resources to perform a complete market scan, and bank's publicity is presumably related to their market share.

---

[6] According to an empirical study by the Federal Deposit Insurance Corporation (2012), this seems to be the most common occasion for bank switches.

44

4.6.2 Federal government

As stated in the chapter Economic basics, public customers usually do not contact banks directly for credit. In the simulation model, the federal government offers bills at the asset market, which all market participants then (maybe) buy. At the moment, this has no further implications model wise in the sense, that the borrowed money does not affect the model in any way (except the banks borrowing the money). The money is taken off the market and does not influence any other model element. Theoretically, the federal government should also be able to default, but that is another research question. The amount of bill offerings is taken from the statistics by the U.S. Department of the Treasury (2013).

4.7 The Federal Reserve System (Fed)

The Federal Reserve's model in this simulation is fairly simple, since it is not a real agent. In a completed simulation concept, there would also be, of course, the possibility to extend this part into a real agent with perception and environment manipulation. And provided that the simulation was able to generate endogenous crises, it could also be an interesting research question to test effects of different policies to the market. But this is a different question, that is not in the perimeter of this thesis.

For the time being, the model replays the real actions of the federal reserve in the relevant years. The discount rates, reserve requirements for banks, interest on required (and excess) reserve balances can be read from the Fed's official data. The federal funds rate works a bit differently, because it is not simply set, but derives from the actions of the market participants. The Fed can, however, influence this rate by open market operations, which means it can buy or sell (mostly government) securities. The model logic does this according to data in the Fed's official historical balance sheet. It calculates the difference of government bill holdings for each month and commences the implied open market operations (buy bills, if difference positive, sell if negative), spreading the resulting acquirement or selling evenly across the month, in order to not induce shocks itself.

4.8 Information market

The information market is an explicit representation of information acquisition costs within an agent based simulation model, enabling, but also regulating the availability of intelligence

(Wilmans, 2013).

It holds pieces of information, which are, in some way, traded. Model elements can publish them automatically. For instance, if a business customer misses an interest payment, the bank agent that notices this, may put an information item onto the information market (free of charge). The federal reserve system model publishes an information about the general direction (down, same, up) of parameters or planned open market operations a few days (simulation time) before the actual change happens.

Information publishing model elements are responsible for setting realistic "prices" for the offered information item. The currency of this market is man hours. The price represents the effort for one person, to acquire and fully understand the information bit in question. Offered information can then be "bought" by other simulation elements. In this very basic version, the information's quality and reliability are not modeled, but its originator is documented. Information consuming model elements can define freely, how much currency they own and the rules under which they are refilled. The man hours do not play any other role than modeling effort on the buyer's side. The invested hours are only checked at purchasing time as to whether they are sufficient to retrieve the information.

The system is relatively simple, but should already allow modelers to research questions such as the distribution of statements and rumors, as well as their effects on the market. The trading branches of banks and hedge funds are mostly consumers of the information, while the federal reserve system, bank's loan retailers and corporate credit customers are more likely to produce information items.

The currently available information items are listed as

- Application for credit
- Dismissal of credit application
- Missed interest payment
- Default
- Positive profit expectation
- Negative profit expectation
-

The list could be expanded further, if there are more useful topics. Of course, for every information item, there is some additional information, that has to be provided. The originator was mentioned and is a common feature of every item. The rest ins context sensitive, e.g. the model element that missed an interest payment is attached to the corresponding item.

5 Realization of the simulation

5.1 Realization goal

The main goal of this project was to experiment with my economic model. This happens in order to test its validity. It has to be noticed, that due to the simulation model's incompleteness, the realization is everything but finished. The component's interfaces are only partly defined and thus not presented here. However, the general software structure is presumably very insensitive to the planned changes and will stay the same, until the simulation is finished.

5.2 Means of goal achievement

To reach the main goal, there are some features that the simulation software should have, which are:

- Correct model implementation

- Manageable scenarios

- (automatic) calibration of model's parameters

- Useful display of simulation results

- Validation of simulation results

5.3 Software components and general structure

5.3.1 Overview

On the top level, the application has three components: the simulation core, the calibration component and the statistics component. When expressed in the QUASAR interface classification, the components are all connected via A_x interfaces. Entities across components are also referenced directly. This decision would have horrible implications if one was to distribute or

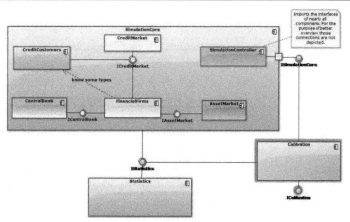

Figure 5.1: overview of components

extend this software significantly. The advantages, compared to more decoupled solutions, however, are directness, a simpler structure and increased (single computer) system execution speed. Since the software is not supposed to be distributed over multiple computers, or used for longer than the experiments for this thesis, I decide to accept those disadvantages.

5.3.2 Simulation Core

The simulation core implements the economic model. Inside, the coordinator orchestrates the execution of the simulation by ticking the included components in a defined order. Namely the ticked components are the CentralBanks, CreditCustomers and FinancialFirms component. This is in contrast to the passive components; the Asset- and the CreditMarket component. They are rather manipulated by the depended components, instead of ticking themselves.

Active Components

Active components are components that hold and calculate the model's actors. They all have a similar design: They define public entities, which represent elements of the functional model, as well as some internal logic. The logic revolves mostly around ticking order, since most interaction logic is contained within the model's actors themselves. In contrast to the information system approach, they are not persistent objects, saved somewhere. They rather live only in the RAM, to the simulation end at most. All existent entities in a simulation run are hold in a temporary storage. Finally, there is the controller that regulates the internal execution by, for example ticking entities in a reasonable order.

CentralBank   This is one of the simulation core's active components. It holds the implementations of the model's central banks. Currently that only includes the Federal Reserve System.

CreditCustomers   This is also an active component. The entities managed here are all credit customers in the model.

FinancialFirms   This is the simulation core's last active component. It implements all model elements that are member of the financial sector. At the moment this includes banks and hedge funds. Since the financial firms have to know their customers, there is an implicit dependency on some classes of the CreditCustomers component.

SimulationController

The simulation controller is the only (semi-) technical component. It implements the central point that controls the simulation run. It provides means for

- Loading scenarios from textfiles

- Controlling the run of the simulation

- Retrieving model independent info about the simulation run

Passive Components

CreditMarket   This component implements the stage for interaction between credit customers and banks. It defines most parts of the model that have to do with the creation of loan contracts. Also, it implements the credit market after the model's description. Banks offer different loan contracts from which the credit customers then choose.

AssetMarket   The asset market can be viewed as a rudimentary implementation of programs running at stock exchanges all over the world. Potential traders of financial assets can place asks and bids to the system. The algorithm inside will then try to match them in a way that the asking trader always gets the best possible deal. According to the model, the tradable assets are all financial assets, not only stocks.

5.3.3 Statistics

As the name already suggests, this component implements all statistics used. All model components pass data-sets during simulation runs, which the component then persists. The saved data can either be accessed directly, or one can get refined and aggregated values from the component.

5.3.4 Calibration

This component is responsible for the automatic calibration of the simulation. It tests multiple simulations with varying parameters using the simulation controller, checking their outputs via the statistics component. The goal is to optimize the simulation's parameters so that the output fits optimally with target values.

6 Outlook

There is some more research to be done, in order to get the simulation model into an executable condition, especially if the goal remains to produce relevant results. Since for a lot of the parts of the model, I found no agent-based models and for others only loosely related models were adapted, not every model part is finished, not even in an oversimplified way. But the model is thought of as a test bed for the examination of assumptions, rather than claiming to have correctly mapped every feature. I plan to advance this model further, hopefully with the help of domain experts, to improve on it.

6.1 Bank agent

The main focus of interest in this model is the behavior of banks. Accordingly, its description is the most detailed one. Yet still not everything is modeled. For example the reader might have noticed, that although most elements of the bank agent do exist and the models behind them are more or less sophisticated, it is not yet specified, how exactly the investment banking agents and the loan retailer take the management's targeted strategic position into account. For a simple first version, this might be done by interpreting the management's strategic target vector dimensions as hard borders and apply them only for new customers. The mortgage risk distribution value ($d_{mortgage}$), for example could be a simple upper border for accepting for new applicants, according to the current distribution. Or the investment banking agents could adjust its deals for every single deal to stay at the management's debt-to-equity-ratio (r_{de}). However, this ignores many effects, that in reality are there, for example that the bank's different parts' ratios add up to an overall ratio, allowing real banks to have differences within their sections. Or that a bank may already have regular customers, who it might need to cancel contracts with in order to reach a management's requirement.

A really important model element that is missing for completion is a derivatives retail section in the bank agent. So far, existing assets could be traded on the stock market, there are bank's and hedge fund's trading sections potentially trying to buy any good at the asset market. But to my knowledge, there is no model yet that describes how the retailers of bank's own derivatives behave, especially not in a multi-agent simulation setting. For a simple first version, it might suffice to "simply" put all sold mortgage loans, in regular intervalls, in a Collateralized Debt Obligation (CDO) structure, let banks offer all of them at the asset market and calculate the results. As to what extent this approach fits to the real-life situation at the relevant time has to be determined.

6.2 Credit customers

The business customers do not yet have a model on how they generate realistic demand for credit out of themselves. Even if effects such as business success, consumer relations, overall credit level and others are left out. There are many ways, how this could be approached. The simplest form would be a stochastic process, similar to that in the private household agent. Business success and thus greater demand for credit would then be determined by a random value maybe with a growth restriction.

A more realistic version might be to allow the predetermination of businesse's "paths" of developments and select them with a realistic distribution over the various agents at initialization time. A path in this context would mean a function of credit demand over time, that is defined before the simulation. One would need different characteristics like "steady cash cow" (slow, monotonous increase) or "exploding" start up with more than linear development or "fast rise with sudden crash".

However, the path solution is even less of a "real" agent than the idiosyncratic, stochastic version. A mid-term goal should be, to incorporate a real agent based model on that end of the global simulation model as well. It could try to emulate a "real economy" with good production, rendition of services and consumption. This would be a completion to a "model" economy with all parts represented at least extremely simplified. If that happened, a lot of the processes, which are momentarily decoupled from effects that economists would anticipate, could be researched further. Employment and wage, government spending and credit demand, as well as corporate development are believed to be tightly coupled, although still differing views exist, on what the true nature of these couplings is.

6.3 Risk management

The most underrepresented element in the model is risk management. It is an own course of study for the various market segments from private credit applicants, over corporate credit and bank's or hedge fund's overall risk management, to the asset trading theories.

This is the reason for many unfinished parts in the model. To approximate realistic conditions, many model parts must have at least a basic form of risk estimation. While some models are publicly available and well documented, more effort is necessary to incorporate them into this simulation model. Furthermore, some essential risk models are not publicly available. As far as I know, the FICO score algorithm, on which banks heavily rely on when determining consumer credit risk, is a business secret of the company that issued it (Fair Isaac Corporation). In fact, it is not guaranteed, that all banks use the same one, all the time. Whatever the real case is, one would either have to reverse-engineer an algorithm that at least approximates the original one from the publicly available information about factors and weighting - or use another one, that may be documented in research papers.

Many other model elements (and especially the connections between those) rely on risk models. In the bank management agent decision process is mentioned, that different strategies have a risk cost, that is taken into account when making decisions. The function, that calculates this risk cost according to the bank's current position and the strategy at hand, has yet to be defined. This part is one the most important areas of focus in the next steps of the model evolution.

6.4 Historic data versus agent

Some model elements, such as the federal government and the federal reserve system, to name a some, are not yet agents. This is done purposefully at the moment, on one hand to have real-world references within the model, which makes it easier to compare simulated values with real world ones from the simulated time. If the environment was realistic and the simulation model produced results comparable to real-life ones with as few parameters as possible, it would be an indicator that one is at the right track. On the other hand, simulation models for many of the other elements are only now slowly emerging. So, to be able to limit the model's domain at least a bit and focus on the main parts, it is simply easier to rely on historical data at some spots.

However this implies, that the model at the time is only able to simulate a relatively limited time frame, for which such historic data is available. Alternatively, one would have to provide the simulation with estimations of future developments from other sources. Given the simulation model's complexity, it will be a challenge, to produce credible results even for the limited time frame for that data is available. Since the questioned time is from 2000 to 2007, this not yet a problem. But should the model give realistic results for that time span, it would be of course the next step to validate it against predictions for the future. For central banking simulation there some agent-based propositions, such as Williams & Eidenbenz (2013).

6.5 Realization, experiments

The whole purpose of an agent-based model is to experiment with it, in order to improve on its assumptions and models, until they can be validated. This part is not even started yet, due to the incompleteness of the simulation model. The actual implementation of the finished model is a necessary, but relatively small set of work, that I intend to proceed with in the future. To attempt calibration and validation of a dynamically complete version this model will pose more interesting research questions. There are useful concepts for parameter space examination and sensitivity analysis, such as an active design of experiment process via a nearly orthogonal latin hypercube with the simulation parameter as the hypercube's dimensions (Oeffner, 2008).

7 Conclusion

I have built wide parts of a simulation model that, once finished, can serve as a platform for domain experts in combination with computer science professionals, to test agent-based economics theories. It incorporates some ACE concepts in complete model parts and presents a foundation for the insertion of more. The high degree of bank's interconnections with practically every part of the economy makes it necessary, to simulate a lot of those other participants more or less realistically.

This is a chance to come closer to a "complete" economic model (from which this model is still far away) as well as a display of the most important disadvantage that agent based models have in comparison to other approaches. Which is, as also Oeffner (2008) mentions, that they have to be dynamically complete in order to be executed by a computer. While this requires models to be "complete" explanations for every possible situation, it also makes it significantly harder for model developers to test parts of the model, before it is complete.

This being said, I have to conclude that the goal of the thesis was met only partly. Although this model is (to my knowledge) the first one that at least attempted to describe the behavior of banks and the resulting consequences within real market conditions (instead of only picking an extremely abstract sub part), it is not complete enough to present simulation results.

Nevertheless, the existence of a nearly finished model might help further research (including my own) to advance on its basis.

Bibliography

Anufriev, Mikhail, & Hommes, Cars H. 2012. Evolutionary Selection of Individual Expectations and Aggregate Outcomes in Asset Pricing Experiments. *American Economic Journal: Microeconomics*, **4**(4), 35–64.

Arthur, W. Brian. 1994. Inductive Reasoning and Bounded Rationality. *The American Economic Review*, 406–411.

Arthur, W. Brian, Holland, John H., LeBaron, Blake, Palmer, Richard, & Taylor, Paul. 30.11.1996. *Asset Pricing Under Endogenous Expectations in an Artificial Stock Market*. Santa Fe.

Basu, N., Pryor, R. J., Quint, T., & Arnold, T. 2001. *Aspen: A microsimulation model of the economy*.

Benes, Jaromir, & Kumhof, Michael. 2012. *The Chicago Plan Revisited IMF Working Paper 13/202; August 2012*.

Brunnermeier, Markus K. 2009. Deciphering the Liquidity and credit crunch 2007-08. 77–100.

Carlton, Dennis W. 1983. Equilibrium Fluctuations when Price and Delivery Lag Clear the Market: Paper. *The Bell Journal of Economics*, **14**(2), 561–572.

Cincotti, Silvano, Raberto, Marco, & Teglio, Andrea. 2010. Credit Money and Macroeconomic Instability in the Agent-based Model and Simulator Eurace. *Economics: The Open-Access, Open-Assessment E-Journal*.

Colander, David, Föllmer, Hans, Haas, Armin, Goldberg, Michael, Juselius, Katarina, Kirman, Alan, Lux, Thomas, & Sloth, Brigitte. 2009. *The Financial Crisis: More is Different: Working Paper*.

Die Zeit. 2011-11-22. Banken leihen sich untereinander kaum noch Geld. *Die Zeit*.

Federal Deposit Insurance Corporation. 2012. *2011 FDIC National Survey of Unbanked and Underbanked Households*.

Federal Reserve Bank St. Louis. 2013. *CMDEBT / GDP * 100.* `http://research.` `stlouisfed.org/fred2/graph/?graph_id=136424&category_id=` `7519#`. Last checked: 2013-11-11.

Federal Reserve Board. 16.03.2006. *H.6 Money Stock Measures.* `http://www.` `federalreserve.gov/releases/H6/20060316/`. Last checked: 2013-09-15.

Financial Stability Board. 2011. Policy Measures to Address Systemically Important Financial Institutions.

Fishman-Lapin, Julie. 2006. Prophet of Doom? Darien market bear says U.S. investors' ship is sinking: S. F1, F6.

Hanson, Robin. 2003. Combinatorial Information Market Design. *Information Systems Frontiers*, 107–119.

Hommes, Cars. 2006a. Interacting agents in finance. *New Palgrave Dictionary of Economics*, **2006**(2), 1–10.

Hommes, Cars H. 2006b. Chapter 23 Heterogeneous Agent Models in Economics and Finance. **2**, 1109–1186.

LeBaron, Blake. 2006. Agent-Based Computational Finance. *Pages 1188–1233 of*: Tesfatsion, Leigh, & Judd, Kenneth L. (eds), *Handbook of Computational Economics*, vol. 2.

Leijonhufvud, A. 2006. Agent-based macro. *Handbook of Computational Economics*, 1625–1637.

Nutting, Rex. 2006-08-23. Recession will be nasty and deep, economist says. *The Wall Street Journal*.

Oeffner, Marc. 2008. *Agent–Based Keynesian Macroeconomics: An Evolutionary Model Embedded in an Agent-Based Computer Simulation.* Ph.D. thesis, Julius–Maximilians–Universität Würzburg, Würzburg.

Pasha, Shaheen. 2006. Banks' love affair with hedge funds: Large banks are eager to manage their own hedge funds, despite recent blowups like Amaranth. *CNN Money*.

Posner, Richard A. 1998. Rational Choice, Behavioral Economics, and the Law. *Stanford Law Review*, 1551–1575.

Reuters. 29.02.2012. *Top investment bank revenues fell 17 pct in 2011.*

Robertson, Duncan A. 2003. Agent-Based Models of a Banking Network as an Example of a Turbulent Environment: The Deliberate vs. Emergent Strategy Debate Revisited. *EMERGENCE*, 56–71.

Simon, Herbert Alexander. 1957. *Models of Man.* New York: John Wiley and Sons, Inc.

Sorkin, Andrew Ross. 2007. The Biggest Hedge Funds? Investment Banks: DealBook. *New York Times.*

Thurner, Stefan. 2011. *systemic financial risk: agent based models to understand the leverage cycle on national scales and its consequences.*

Traub, Amy, & Ruetschlin, Catherine. 22.05.2012. *The plastic safety net: Findings from the 2012 national survey on credit card debt of low- and middle-income households.* New York.

U.S. Department of the Treasury. 2013. *Treasury Bulletin: Profile of the Economy Financial Operations International Statistics Special Reports.* Washington D.C.

U.S. Securities and Exchange Commission. 25.07.2013. *Annual Staff Report Relating to the Use of Data Collected from Private Fund Systemic Risk Reports.*

Wikipedia Foundation. 2013. *Information market.* http://en.wikipedia.org/wiki/Information_market. Last checked: 2013-07-05.

Williams, Sean, & Eidenbenz, Stephan. 2013. *Themis-1: An Agent-Based Model of a Modern Monetary Reserve System.* Los Alamos.

Wilmans, Jason T. 2013. *An overview of Multi-Agent Based Models with Bounded Rationality.*

Zarnowitz, Victor. 1962. Unfilled Orders, Price Changes, And Business Fluctuations. *The Review of Economics and statistics.*

www.ingramcontent.com/pod-product-compliance
Lightning Source LLC
La Vergne TN
LVHW042348060326
832902LV00006B/466